JOHANNES BRAHMS
From the silverpoint drawing by J. B. Laurens

JOHANNES BRAHMS

Complete Sonatas and Variations for Solo Piano

EDITED BY

EUSEBIUS MANDYCZEWSKI

THE VIENNA GESELLSCHAFT DER MUSIKFREUNDE EDITION

_____

Dover Publications, Inc., New York

CONTENTS

Published in Canada by General Publishing Company, Ltd.,
30 Lesmill Road, Don Mills, Toronto, Ontario.
Published in the United Kingdom by Constable and Company,
Ltd., 10 Orange Street, London WC 2.

This Dover edition, first published in 1971, is an unabridged
republication of Volume (*Band*) 13, entitled *Sonaten und Variationen
für Klavier zu zwei Händen*, of the collection *Johannes Brahms; Sämtliche
Werke; Ausgabe der Gesellschaft der Musikfreunde in Wien*, originally
published by Breitkopf & Härtel, Leipzig (n.d.; Editor's Preface to
Volume 13 dated Autumn, 1927).
The Editor's Preface (*Revisionsbericht*) and the table of contents
appear here only in English translation, which was prepared specially
for this Dover edition.

International Standard Book Number: 0-486-22650-6
Library of Congress Catalog Card Number: 73-116829

Manufactured in the United States of America
Dover Publications, Inc.
180 Varick Street
New York, N.Y. 10014

EDITOR'S PREFACE

SONATA, Op. 1.

BASIC TEXTS FOR THE PRESENT EDITION:

1. The composer's original manuscript, in the Vienna National-bibliothek. Fourteen oblong leaves, the first three and the last three leaves twelve-staff piano music paper, the eight inserted leaves twelve-staff paper for voice and piano accompaniment, used upside down. Title on the first page: "Vierte Sonate f. d. Piano." Page 25 (at the end): "Fine. Joh. Kreisler jun." No date, no signature.

2. The composer's personal copy of the first edition, in the collection of the Gesellschaft der Musikfreunde, Vienna. This edition was published in 1853 with the title: "Sonate (*C* dur) für das Pianoforte componirt und Joseph Joachim zugeeignet von Johannes Brahms. Op. 1. Eigenthum der Verleger. Leipzig, bei Breitkopf und Härtel." Publication number 8833.

COMMENTS:

Brahms later made small alterations in pencil in his personal copy, evidently for a possible new edition of his youthful work. Thus we follow this basic text throughout. Page 7, measures 7 and 6 from the bottom, the first edition indicates for the left hand:

Page 10, measure 8 from the bottom, the last note of the triplets is given as F_1; page 23, measure 7 from the bottom, the second note in the left hand is E; page 24, in the sixth 9/8 measure, the last note in the left hand is g; page 25, measure 4 from the bottom, the first chord in the right hand is exactly like the last (which, of course, is under the 8·····); page 27, at the entry of the 6/8 measure there is the tempo alteration "*Presto agitato ma non troppo*"; page 28, line 4, measures 1, 2, 5 and 6, the first chords in the left hand are as in line 3, measure 5; finally, the closing chord in the left hand is:

If through these alterations, slight as they are, we obtain the definitive version of the work, then through a comparison between the original manuscript and the first edition, which was surely carefully checked by the composer, we learn something about its creation, and first of all, that it was not the *first* piano sonata Brahms composed. Moving on to particulars: page 2, line 4, measure 2, the manuscript indicates for the right hand:

and, correspondingly, on page 8, line 2, measure 4, the same chords a third higher; page 2, measure 4 from the bottom, the left hand rests on the fourth quarter note; page 3, measure 1, the second half of the measure in the left hand is the same as the first half; page 3, measure 5, the second chord in the left hand lacks the fourth and the ninth; page 4, line 3, the manuscript gives measures 2–4 as:

Page 4, measure 6 from the bottom, the left hand begins:

Page 5, line 2, measures 1–4, the left hand has:

Page 6, measures 2–6, the right hand continues the progression in sixths and octaves (as in measure 1) *pp dolcissimo* and *portamento* until measure 7; page 6, line 4, measure 3, the left hand has:

and in the next line:

Page 6, next-to-last measure, in the manuscript, as a change from the immediately preceding passage, the horn-like passage ceases and the left hand has:

Page 7, line 2, measures 3 and 4, the right-hand chords have no *b*-flat.

Page 7, line 4, measure 2, the first chord in the left hand is an octave lower, without arpeggio or tenth; likewise two measures later, a half tone higher.

Page 9, line 4, measures 5 ff., the eighth notes in the left hand are *staccato* throughout, but the right hand's answering octaves four measures later have an alternation with *legato* (as printed).

Page 9, measure 5 from the bottom, the last chord in the right hand has g^2 instead of a^2; in the next measure the tie which originally connected the bottom notes of the two chords in the left hand (f) is clearly deleted (apparently because of the ff).

Page 10, line 4, measure 1, the second triplet in the left hand is $f\,e\,f$ (not $e\,g\,f$); in the next measure the last triplet note, along with the slur which ends there, has a *staccato* dot, and likewise two measures later (the apparent intention being to emphasize the bass note).

Page 11, line 3, the last right-hand chord is simultaneous with the left hand, instead of coming in later.

Page 11, next-to-last measure, the third sixteenth note from the end is in unison with the upper voice f^2 (compare the fourth measure from the bottom).

Page 13, line 5, measure 2, the last eighth note in the upper voice of the left hand is c^1 and similarly two measures later b, but two measures after that g.

Page 14, measure 4:

Page 14, line 3, measure 3, the eighth notes in the right hand are $g\,a\,b\,c\,e$ (not $g\,b\,c\,d\,e$); in the last measure of the same line, the final note of the melody is b in the right hand and the left-hand chord has a as a third. Page 14, measure 5 from the bottom in the left hand is:

Page 15, line 5, measure 3, the right hand has the fingering:

3	4	5	4	5		4
2	1	3	2	1		2

and, correspondingly, in measure 5:

3	4	5	4	5		5
2	1	3	2	1		3
						2

Page 16, measure 5, the right-hand eighth notes are $b\,c\,c\sharp\,d\sharp\,e\,g\sharp$, corresponding to the parallel passage on page 14 mentioned above; page 17, line 3, measures 5 and 6 lack the sustained bass note g in the left hand; likewise page 18, line 2, measures 5 and 6; the footnote on page 17 occurs in the manuscript; the closing section of the Scherzo, beginning page 19, line 2, measure 3, appears in the manuscript as:

Page 20, measure 1, the left hand has:

Page 20, measure 3, the right-hand *sf* chords have no g^2.

Page 20, line 3, measures 3 ff.:

Page 21, line 5, the last right-hand chord in measure 1 and the first (same) chord in measure 2 lack the e^1; likewise four measures

later; the same is true on page 22 at the entry of the *a tempo*, but not at the subsequent *cresc. poco a poco* four measures thereafter.

Page 22, line 5, measure 1 has a *sost.*

Page 23, line 2, measure 2, the fourth and fifth eighth notes in the right hand are crossed out in the manuscript, but restored in the first edition; the same is true of the a^1 in the last right-hand chord on page 24, line 3, measure 2.

Page 24, line 4, in the third beat of measure 1 the left hand must also play a ♩. *d.*

Page 25, line 3, measures 6 and 7 form only one measure with a ⌒ and the indication "*lunga pausa*"; the next measure (9/8) is marked "*leggiero e delicato.*"

Page 26, measures 7–9, the chords are more full:

Page 27, measure 5 is marked "*molto agitato e più mosso.*"

Page 27, line 2, measure 3, the first right-hand chord is $a\sharp^2\ c\sharp^3\ e^3$, and correspondingly line 3, measure 2, the same chord a half tone higher.

Page 28, line 4, measures 1, 2, 5 and 6, the first left-hand chords as in line 3, measure 5; line 5, measures 2 and 3 appear as:

Finally, it should be noted in general that the manuscript's *fz*, which occurs particularly frequently in this work, is given as *sf* in the first edition; that both basic texts usually allow the performer to decide when "*Ped*" and "*una corda*" should be released; and that the *pf* (seldom used elsewhere) stands not for *piano forte*, but for *poco forte*.

SONATA, Op. 2.

BASIC TEXTS FOR THE PRESENT EDITION:

1. A handwritten copy by Brahms, in the collection of Breitkopf & Härtel, Leipzig, with the title (written by Brahms): "Sonate für's Pianoforte von Joh⁸ Brahms. op. 2." A careful copy, on which the composer had to change very little. Division into plates shows that it was used as engraving copy for the first edition.

2. The composer's personal copy of the first edition, in the collection of the Gesellschaft der Musikfreunde, Vienna. This edition was published in 1853 with the title: "Sonate Fis moll für das Pianoforte componirt und Frau Clara Schumann verehrend zugeeignet von Johannes Brahms. Op. 2. Leipzig, bei Breitkopf & Härtel." Publication number 8834. Contains later corrections by Brahms.

3. A copy, also corrected by Brahms, of the 1880 Breitkopf & Härtel edition of his "Pianoforte-Werke zu zwei Händen,"

containing opus numbers 1, 2, 4, 9, 10 and 24 (publication number 13 598), in the collection of Frau Flore Luithlen-Kalbeck, Vienna.

COMMENTS:

Brahms's corrections in basic texts 2 and 3 are partly identical and partly supplement each other. To all appearances they were done at various times.

Page 1, the *staccato* in the *ff* is indicated by accents, whereas dots are used on page 6, though surely no difference is intended. Brahms has a general tendency to use accents for *staccato* in *ff* and *f*, dots in *p* and *pp*, and this is in accord with the customary meaning of these marks. But he does not apply them pedantically.

Page 4, measures 4 and 5, in basic text 1 the first quarter beat has a triad (not a chord of the sixth) on *c♯*, and the chord of the seventh does not come in until the *f✳*. The same is true of the parallel passage at the bottom of page 8. Thus the alteration was first made for the printed edition.

Page 12, measures 2, 4, 5, 6, 10, 12, 14 and 16, basic text 1 and the first edition have *ff* where we have followed the handwritten correction in basic texts 2 and 3 in printing *f ＜ ff*.

Page 13, the last three bars of the right hand in basic text 1 have only the upper voice.

Page 15, measure 8, basic text 1 reads:

Page 16, for measures 7 and 8 and the first half of measure 9, Brahms made a notation "*più facile*" in basic text 3, but did not write it out. It may be assumed that he intended to simplify this passage by omitting the notes for the thumb of the right hand. At any rate he would have wanted them engraved in smaller notation, as in the similar cases in the sonatas Op. 1 and Op. 5 (pages 17 and [59]5 of the present volume). Possibly connected with this intended "*più facile*" is Brahms's later revision, in basic text 3, of the next section in the right hand; we have printed this revision here as being his definitive wish. The original version of this passage, as shown in all the basic texts, was, beginning with the double bar:

In both basic texts (2 and 3) Brahms alters the left-hand part in the last of these measures, so that it is played an octave higher.

Page 16, line 4, measure 1, the *E*-flat of the first octaves in the left hand was a later change by Brahms; it was originally *E* and appears thus in all the basic texts.

Page 17, last line, measure 1, the ♮ in front of the e^1 under the "*pesante*" is lacking in all the basic texts, but is surely self-evident in view of Brahms's healthy sensibilities, so alien to all sentimentality. In the last measure on this page, all the basic texts give the last left-hand note as merely $c\sharp^1$; in basic text 3 Brahms added the $c\sharp^1$ tied to the preceding note.

Page 18, measure 7, in the basic texts the terminal notes

(*Nachschlag*) after the trill are not written out, but indicated by *tr♯*. We have written them out for clarity here and in similar self-evident cases (also page 17, line 5, measure 5); it should be noted that Brahms allowed trills without *Nachschlag* only very exceptionally.

Page 19, line 4, measure 2, in the basic texts the last quarter beat was originally a diminished triad on *f♯*, which Brahms later changed.

Page 20, measure 3, the absence of the ♯ in front of the *f²* in the second right-hand chord is surely only an oversight of Brahms's. Cf. page 24, line 5, measure 2.

Page 21, line 6, measures 1–3, the original version of the left-hand part, still recognizable in basic text 1:

was simplified by Brahms for the first edition.

Page 24, measures 1 and 3, all the basic texts have a ♯ in front of the seventh eighth note in the left hand (*d*), but after the ✕ in front of the third eighth note (also *d*) this is hard to understand, since Brahms always marks the change from double sharp to single sharp with a ♮♯. The right-hand part in this passage also supplies evidence that the ✕· is to be retained, and the immediately following measures 2, 4 and 5 should also be compared.

Page 26, line 3, measure 2, in all the basic texts the ascending scale from *d♯¹* to *c♯³* was originally complete, like the scale in the preceding measure; in texts 2 and 3 Brahms later deleted the *b²* in this scale.

––––––––

SONATA, Op. 5.

BASIC TEXTS FOR THE PRESENT EDITION:

1. The composer's original manuscript, in the collection of Dr. Karl Freiherr von Vietinghoff, Berlin; fifteen vertical leaves of sixteen-staff music paper with the title: "Sonate (F moll) für das Pianoforte componirt und der Frau Gräfin Ida von Hohenthal geb. Gräfin von Scherr-Thoss zugeeignet von Johannes Brahms. Op. 5." At the end: "Kreisler jun." The manuscript was used as engraving copy.
2. The proofs of the first edition, in the same collection, which the composer made much use of for additions, alterations, expression marks and the like.
3. The composer's personal copy of the first edition, in the collection of the Gesellschaft der Musikfreunde, Vienna. This edition was published with exactly the same title that appears on the manuscript; the year was 1854, the publisher Bartholf Senff, Leipzig, the publication number 101.

COMMENTS:

Basic text 2 shows how conscientiously, indeed with what painful scrupulousness, the composer went about the polishing of his work, even after the engraving was completed. And even in later years, after the work was disseminated in print, we find him making further refinements and improvements in the personal copy.

Page 1, measures 1, 2, 3, the personal copy shows the improvement of altering the *staccato* eighth notes which open the measures into accented quarter notes; we have made this change consistent in the parallel passages as well, since this was doubtless the intention.

Page 1, next-to-last measure, in the manuscript the second left-hand chord is *c f a-flat f¹*; in the same measure the personal copy deletes the *arpeggio* sign from the last two right-hand chords.

Page 3, lines 1 and 2, the tempo alternation follows the personal copy.

Page 3, line 3, measure 5, the first edition, like its predecessors, gives *g♯* as the second sixteenth note in the right hand, *g* in the left hand. The corrections in the personal copy at first show us the composer in doubt about the way to resolve this; first he decides to give the left hand *g♯* along with the right hand, then he decides on *g*, adding expressly "♮*g* above and below."

Page 4, the last two bars read in the manuscript:

This was also originally engraved, but was already changed in the proofs of the first edition (basic text 2).

Page 5, all the basic texts have the footnote.

Page 5, line 5, measure 3, all the basic texts also show an *a²* in the last right-hand chord; it is deleted in the personal copy (duplication of the leading tone in the bass).

Page 6, measure 6, the second right-hand chord (as on page 2, measure 6) is a six-four chord in the manuscript, but was changed in first proofs.

Page 6, the "*più vivo e rubato*" below does not yet appear in the manuscript.

Page 7, line 6, measure 1, the manuscript does not yet show change of meter and the same chords occur on eighth notes (change made in first proofs).

Page 8, line 3, measures 4 and 5, in the manuscripts the left hand has:

and the hands do not cross. The same is true on page 12, measures 4 and 5.

Page 9, line 2, measure 1, in all basic texts the fourth sixteenth note in the left hand is *a*-flat, in the next measure ♮*a*; both are corrected in the personal copy.

Page 9, line 6, measures 4 and 5, the lower double flat in the left hand is from a change made in the personal copy, whereas the other texts give *c*-flat and *c*. The same is true on page 10, line 5, measures 3 and 4.

Page 12, third measure from the bottom, in the manuscript and first proofs the sixth sixteenth note is *g¹*; in the first edition it is *a*-flat¹ and was perhaps not changed back merely through oversight.

Page 13, line 3, the pedal mark follows the basic texts.

Page 14, line 5, measure 3, the half note *b*-flat is the personal copy's alteration for the quarter notes *b*-flat *a*-natural of the other texts.

Page 15, the manuscript originally read "*Allegro molto energico.*"

Page 17, line 5, measure 6, in the manuscript the second left-hand chord is the same as the first.

Page 19, line 3, measure 5, originally the 8*va·····* mark continued another eight measures up to the *ff*, and from that point the end of the Trio read:

We follow the correction in the personal copy.

Page 26, line 4, measure 9, the manuscript has *f* (forte), but this is changed in the proofs.

Page 27, line 2, measures 3 and 4, in the manuscript the right hand has:

This is changed in the proofs.

Page 29, lines 1 and 2, the *cresc.* and *accel.* are derived from the personal copy, as is the *fp* at the *Più mosso.*

Page 30, measures 4, 6, 8 and 10, the left-hand rhythm, given in the manuscript as is changed in the proofs. Likewise:

Page 31, measure 7, the left-hand chord reads

in the manuscript.

Page 32, line 2, measures 3, 4, 5, the manuscript has:

This was also changed in the proofs, and so was originally already engraved. On the other hand, the original ending of the work, beginning page 32, line 4, measure 6, read thus:

but was already altered in the manuscript.

Page 32, line 3, measures 2 and 4 appear thus in all the basic texts: sextolets in place of five eighth notes.

In the proofs this is all pasted over and replaced in handwriting by the passage printed here after the personal copy.

Page 20, the manuscript originally had just "Rückblick" (Backward Glance) and the first twelve measures were repeated.

Page 21, measure 2, the manuscript shows the sign for releasing the pedal in the middle of the measure of rest; the personal copy has it in the second half of the measure.

Page 23, line 2, measure 5, the tremolo in the left hand (*f a*), a third lower in all the basic texts, is a correction from the personal copy.

Page 24, line 2, measures 2–4, the manuscript also has the first note (*e¹*) of the right hand sustained, but this is deleted in the first proofs.

Page 24, line 3, measure 1, the manuscript clearly states "*p leggiero,*" but the first proofs have "*f leggiero,*" a contradiction that was evidently an oversight of the engraver and was apparently not noticed by the composer in his personal copy.

Page 24, the last four measures, and page 25, the first three measures, the basic texts have:

VARIATIONS, Op. 9.

BASIC TEXTS FOR THE PRESENT EDITION:

1. The composer's original manuscript, in the collection of the Gesellschaft der Musikfreunde, Vienna. Eight oblong leaves of twelve-staff music paper, containing three blank pages. On the first page, at the lower right, just: "Frau Clara Schumann in inniger Verehrung von J. B. d. 15 Juni 54." Heading of the composition, which begins on the second page: "Kleine Variationen über ein Tema von Ihm. Ihr zugeeignet." Originally there were only fourteen variations; at the end of the last is written: "Düsseldorf Juni 1854." On a separate sheet, inserted later, are variations 10 and 11 with the bracketed heading "(Rose und Heliotrop haben geduftet)" and the date "Düsseldorf am 12. August 54. J. B."

2. The composer's personal copy of the first edition, in the same collection. This edition was published in 1854 with the title: "Variationen für das Pianoforte über ein Thema von Robert Schumann Frau Clara Schumann zugeeignet von Johannes Brahms. op. 9. Eigenthum der Verleger. Leipzig, Breitkopf & Härtel. Pr. 25 Ngr." Publication number 9001.

3. A copy, corrected by Brahms, of the 1880 Breitkopf & Härtel, Leipzig, edition of his "Pianoforte-Werke zu zwei Händen" (opp. 1, 2, 4, 9, 10, 24), in the collection of Frau Flore Luithlen-Kalbeck, Vienna.

4. The second edition, checked by Brahms, which was published with the same title by N. Simrock G. m. b. H., Berlin and Leipzig.

COMMENTS:

In the manuscript, the double bars at the close of variations 4, 7, 8, 11, 14 and 16 are drawn out into the letter "B" (for Brahms), those of variations 5, 6, 9, 12 and 13 into a "Kr" (for Kreisler). Basic texts 2 and 3 have later pencil corrections by Brahms. Most of these are already incorporated into text 4. We will mention the most important.

Page 1, in the manuscript the second part of the theme has the repeat sign as in Schumann's original ("Bunte Blätter," op. 99). Even "*ad lib. da capo*" was originally added, but was later crossed out.

Page 2, in the manuscript the last (eighth) note in the left hand was originally *c♯* and became *F♯* only in the repeat (page 3, measure 6).

Page 5, measures 12–15, in the manuscript the left-hand octaves do not have the inner voice *c♯*.

Page 5, line 4, measure 5, the first note in the right hand ($A\sharp_1$) is an eighth note followed by an eighth rest.

Page 6, measures 1 and 2 read in the manuscript and first edition:

and correspondingly in the next six measures, as also in the repeat on page 7. The change was first indicated in basic text 3 and even in text 4 it is not yet fully carried out.

Page 6, line 2, measure 2, and line 3, measure 3, the third eighth beat still reads

in the second edition. We follow the very energetically repeated correction in basic text 3.

Page 8, in basic texts 1 and 2 variation 8 has an uninterrupted sextolet accompaniment, as in line 1, measure 3, line 2, measures 1 and 3, etc. The alternation with thirty-second notes in this accompaniment is worked out in writing in basic text 3 and already carried out in text 4. In text 1 the tempo indication of this variation is still "*Andante (non troppo)*."

Page 10, in the manuscript the last measure has a *rit.* which was omitted in the other texts, perhaps with no special intention.

Page 11, line 2, in the manuscript the change in key and meter occurs a measure earlier and variation 11 is marked "*l'istesso tempo*."

Page 13, line 1, no repeat in the manuscript.

Page 14, the manuscript reads "*Poco Andante*."

Page 15, measure 2, the not unnecessary expression mark for the left hand occurs only in the manuscript. The same is true of:

Page 16, the "*Adagio*" for the last variation.

VARIATIONS, OP. 21, NO. 1.

BASIC TEXT FOR THE PRESENT EDITION:

The composer's personal copy of the first edition, in the collection of the Gesellschaft der Musikfreunde, Vienna. This edition was published in 1861 with the title: "Variationen für das Pianoforte componirt von Johannes Brahms op. 21. Nr. 1 über ein eigenes Thema, Preis 2 fr. 25, Nr. 2 über ein ungarisches Lied, 2 fr. Eigenthum des Verlegers, Bonn bei N. Simrock." Publication number 6203.

COMMENTS:

In his personal copy Brahms later corrected a few errors in this somewhat carelessly prepared edition; other passages, even doubtful ones, were not changed.

Page 1, line 3, measure 5, the first melody note in the basic text is b^1.

Page 3, line 2, measure 6, the first note of the middle voice, to be played by the thumb of the right hand, is g^1 in the basic text, altered by Brahms to $f\sharp^1$.

Page 3, line 5, measure 1, the basic text lacks the ♮ in front of the F, even though this measure begins a new line.

Page 7, line 2, measure 3, in the basic text the last note in the upper voice is f^3.

Page 8, line 3, in the basic text the first note for the thumb of the right hand is e^2.

Page 9, the basic text gives no special indication (considering it as self-evident) that variation 10 begins *forte* and the eighth notes in the upper and lower voice of the right hand are to be played *legato*. Nor does it show the ♮ in the last two measures on this page.

Page 10, measure 4, in the first edition the next-to-last sixteenth note is $f\sharp^2$; Brahms changed it later.

VARIATIONS, Op. 21, NO. 2.

BASIC TEXTS FOR THE PRESENT EDITION:

1. The composer's original manuscript, in the Vienna Municipal Library; two oblong leaves of fourteen-staff music paper and two of ten-staff (Köster, Hamburg). Heading: "Variationen über ein ungrisches Lied"; no signature or date. On the last page, in the closing flourish: "Brhms."

2. The composer's personal copy of the first edition; in the collection of the Gesellschaft der Musikfreunde, Vienna.

This edition was published in 1861 with the title given above for Op. 21, No. 1. Publication number 6204.

COMMENTS:

The manuscript was written in very lively and apparently rapid strokes, but is not careless. It was not used as engraving copy for the first edition, but the two texts agree basically. A few expression marks have been added or made more precise in the present edition on the basis of the manuscript. The last measure of the theme and of the first and fifth variations originally had a "*rit.*"; this was deleted in the manuscript. The original "*sost.*" in the last measure of the fourth variation was also deleted in the manuscript, but was restored in the first edition. The *ff* of the first variation is expressly assigned to the left hand in the manuscript, but not in the first edition, apparently because it is self-evident. In the manuscript, variation 5 is marked "*con passione,*" while variation 8 is marked "*ancora poco più lento*" and has a ⌒ on the last quarter note. Variation 9 proves to be a later insertion. In variations 10 and 11 a few left-hand chords are simpler. In the closing section, at the beginning of the B-flat minor there is a "*poco meno presto,*" and a "*Tempo 1mo*" at the end of it. Page 10(124), fourth measure from the end, the first chord in the manuscript is a triad (not a chord of the sixth) and so the left hand is a third lower.

VARIATIONS, Op. 24.

BASIC TEXTS FOR THE PRESENT EDITION:

1. The composer's original manuscript, in the collection of Jerôme Stonborough, Vienna. It has the heading "Variationen für eine liebe Freundin. Joh^s Brahms. Sept. 61," and over the first measure "*Aria di Händel*" with no tempo indication.

2. A copy made by the composer for the publisher—thus also an original manuscript—in the collection of Breitkopf & Härtel, Leipzig. Eleven oblong leaves of fourteen-staff music paper; on the first page the autograph title: "Variationen und Fuge über ein Thema von Händel für das Pianoforte componirt von Johannes Brahms. op. 24." On the second page the heading: "Variationen. Joh^s Brahms." And again "*Aria di Händel*" with no tempo indication. In this manuscript the last (twelfth) leaf is missing; it contained only the last four bars of the final section.

3. The composer's personal copy of the first edition, in the collection of the Gesellschaft der Musikfreunde, Vienna. Basic text 2 was the engraving copy for this edition, which has the same title, in addition to: "Eigenthum der Verleger für alle Länder..Leipzig, Breitkopf & Härtel." Publication number 10448.

4. The copy of the same publishers' "Pianoforte-Werke zu zwei Händen" mentioned above; see Variations, Op. 9.

COMMENTS:

A few corrections marked in the first manuscript are already adopted in the second. The personal copy contains no later notations by Brahms, who overlooked a few engraving errors of this first edition. In basic text 4 he later outlined a small alteration in the piano writing, which we shall have to consider.

Page 3, variation 4, the original *Vivace* became a *risoluto* in the second manuscript.

Page 4, variation 7, originally *molto vivace.*

Page 6, variation 10, also just *vivace* originally.

Page 8, variation 13, originally *Un poco largamente.*

Page 9, variation 14, also originally *vivace.*

Page 10, variation 15, the second manuscript shows an attempt to simplify the right-hand part for the performer, should this be necessary, by omitting the lower voice in the sixteenth-note figure. But this change does not even appear in the first edition.

Page 11, variation 17 originally lacked the *più mosso.*

Page 12, variation 19, originally *molto vivace e leggiero.*

Page 18, measure 4, we follow the correction in basic text 4. All the other basic texts show the original version:

Page 19, beginning line 3, measure 2, basic text 1 shows the original version of the left-hand part:

and its first alteration:

We follow the other texts.

Page 20, last line, basic text 1 shows the original:

VARIATIONS, Op. 35.

BASIC TEXTS FOR THE PRESENT EDITION:

1. The composer's original manuscript, containing both parts of the work, formerly in the collection of Leo Liepmannssohn, Berlin.

2. The composer's original manuscript, containing only the first part, in the collection of Paul Wittgenstein, Vienna; seven oblong leaves of ten-staff piano music paper, without heading or date, the first page blank, on the second page a

blank space for the theme, and immediately thereafter the first variation. On the last side, at the end, the simple signature "Brahms."

3. The composer's original manuscript, containing on one isolated sheet only the first variation of the second part; in the collection of the Gesellschaft der Musikfreunde, Vienna; no heading, signature or date.

4. The composer's personal copy of the first edition, in the same collection. This edition was published in 1866 with the title: "Studien für Pianoforte. Variationen über ein Thema von Paganini, componirt von Johannes Brahms. op. 35. Heft I. Heft II. Eigenthum des Verlegers für alle Länder. Leipzig u. Winterthur, J. Rieter-Biedermann." Publication number 436. a. b.

COMMENTS:

Basic texts 2 and 3 are first drafts, text 1 is the clean copy for the printer. It also contains the theme. All the basic texts have later corrections by Brahms; most of the corrections in the manuscripts were adopted in the first edition, those in the personal copy were done later. Some particulars follow.

Set I. Page 1, basic text 1 has *Presto* for the theme and *Non troppo presto* for the first variation. We follow the first edition.

Page 5, in texts 2 and 4, variation 4 is in 12/16 time; in text 4 it has the indication, somewhat unclear for this meter, $\quarternote = \eighthnote$; we follow text 1 and print the variation—as there stated—"with double note-value, 12/8 time," doing without this tempo indication just as we have done without the $\eighthnote = \quarternote$ for variation 5 which it leads to in text 4.

Page 8, measures 4 and 8 are the same as measures 2 and 6 in all the basic texts; the personal copy changed them later.

Page 11, measures 4, 5 and 6, the small notes are in text 2, not in text 4.

Set II. Page 2, line 3, measure 3, in the manuscript the left hand has to continue the octave leaps on the g♯ as well. We follow the first edition.

Page 9, the fingering for variation 9 is written in in the personal copy.

Page 11, variation 12, for the phrasing in the right hand and the accompaniment in the left we follow the later corrections to this variation in the personal copy.

Page 12, variation 13 shows the fingerings written in in the personal copy. Moreover, for the first six eighth notes in the right hand the personal copy has an "NB" and an optional simplification "5 4 5 4 5 4."

Page 14, line 4, between measures 3 and 4 the manuscript (text 1) originally had the following measures:

Page 15, from line 2, measure 5, to the 6/8 in line 5, in the manuscript this passage also had an "*ossia*," an optional substitution, as follows:

After the cadenza, which was left to the performer, the 6/8 was to begin.

This volume includes the portrait of the youthful Brahms which we owe to Robert Schumann. It shows the composer at the period of the sonatas reprinted here.

Vienna   EUSEBIUS MANDYCZEWSKI
Autumn, 1927

Sonate Nr.1
für Pianoforte

Joseph Joachim zugeeignet

Johannes Brahms, Op. 1
(Veröffentlicht 1853)

Allegro

J.B. 50

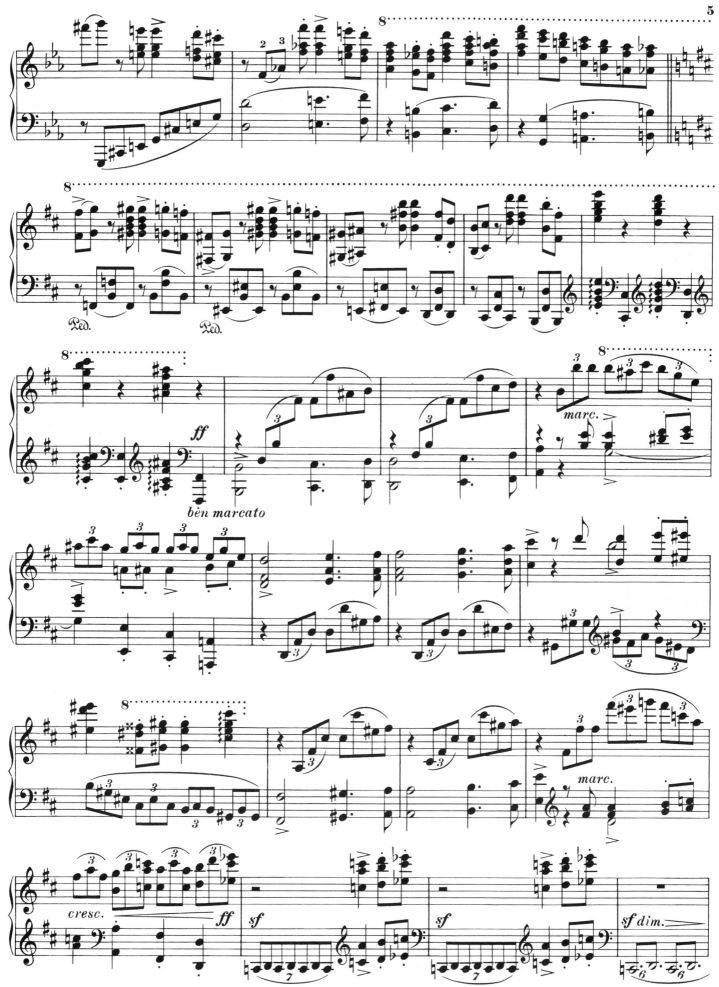

J. B. 50

Più facile

ff largamente

Andante
(Nach einem altdeutschen Minneliede)

Ver_stoh_len geht der Mond auf, blau, blau Blü_me_lein, durch Sil_ber_wölkchen führt sein Lauf:

blau, blau Blü_me_lein. Ro_sen im Tal, Mä_del im Saal, o schönste Ro_sa!

J. B. 50

J. B. 50

Scherzo
Allegro molto e con fuoco

*) Die kleinen Noten können nötigenfalls wegbleiben   J. B. 50

* The smaller notes may be omitted if necessary.

Da Capo il Scherzo senza rep. sin' al Fine

Finale
Allegro con fuoco

28

Sonate Nr.2
für Pianoforte

Frau Clara Schumann verehrend zugeeignet

Allegro non troppo ma energico

Johannes Brahms, Op. 2
(Veröffentlicht 1853)

Andante con espressione

sempre ben marcata ed espress. la melodia

p dolce

cresc.

f rit.

lunga

marcata la melodia

Tempo I

con molt'agitazione

Scherzo
Allegro

Trio

Poco più moderato

Finale

Introduzione
Sostenuto

Allegro non troppo e rubato

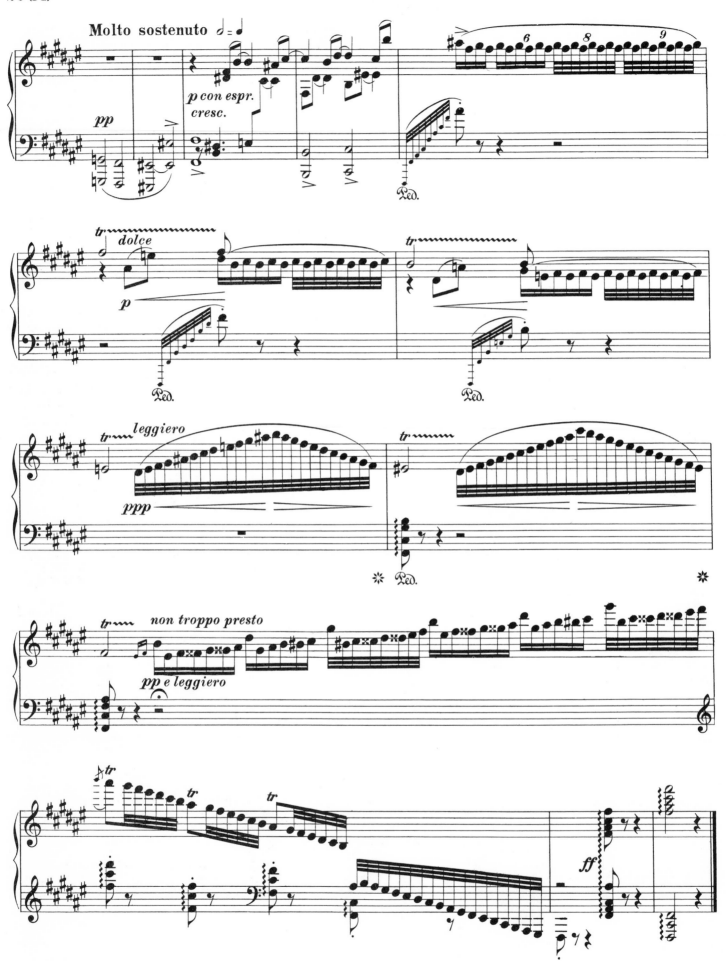

Sonate Nr.3
für Pianoforte

Frau Gräfin von Hohenthal gewidmet

Johannes Brahms, Op.5
(Veröffentlicht 1854)

Allegro maestoso

J.B. 52

*)Die kleinen Noten können nötigenfalls wegbleiben.   J.B.52

* The smaller notes may be omitted if necessary.

Andante

Der Abend dämmert, das Mondlicht scheint,
Da sind zwei Herzen in Liebe vereint
Und halten sich selig umfangen.

Sternau

Poco più lento *Äußerst leise und zart*

sempre Pedale

J. B. 52

Scherzo

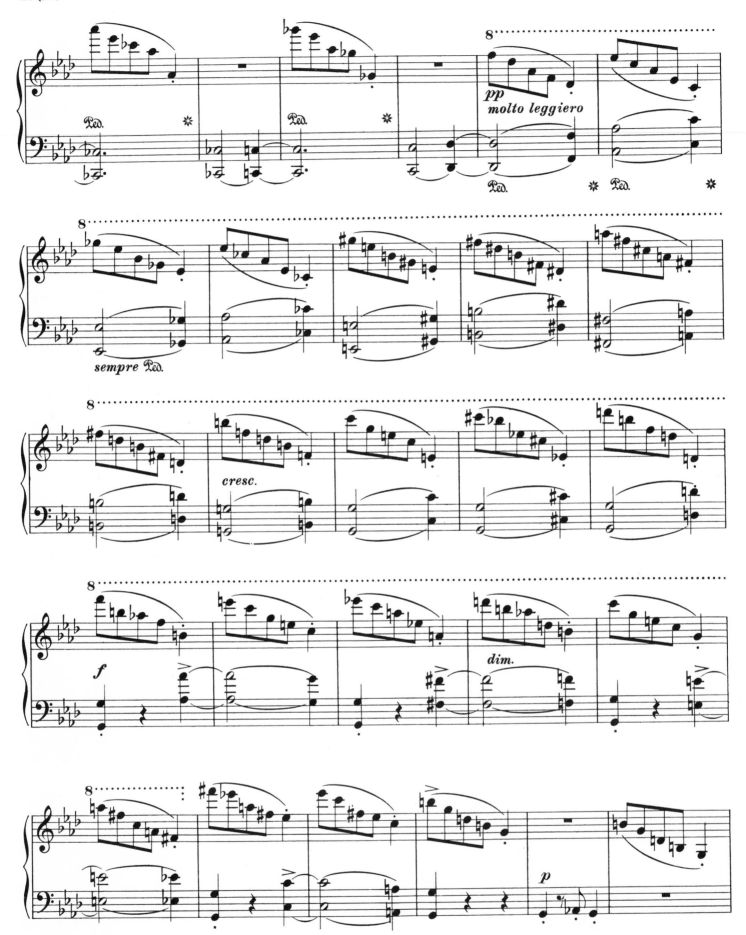

Trio

Dal segno sino al Fine.

Intermezzo
(Rückblick)

Finale

Allegro moderato ma rubato

Variationen

über ein Thema von Robert Schumann für Pianoforte

Frau Clara Schumann zugeeignet

Johannes Brahms, Op.9
(Veröffentlicht 1854)

Thema
Ziemlich langsam

Var. 4

Poco più moto

Var. 5

Allegro capriccioso

Var. 6

Allegro

Var. 7
Andante

Var. 8

Andante (non troppo lento)

Poco Adagio

Var. 12

Allegretto, poco scherzando

Var. 13
Non troppo Presto

Var 14

Andante

Var. 15
Poco Adagio

Var. 16
Adagio

Variationen
über ein eigenes Thema für Pianoforte

Thema
Poco larghetto

Johannes Brahms, Op. 21, Nr. 1
(Veröffentlicht 1861)

Var. 2
Più moto

Tempo di tema

Var. 6
Più moto
espressivo

p legato

Più facile

Var. 7
Andante con moto

Var. 8

Allegro non troppo

Var. 9

Var. 10

Var. 11

Variationen

über ein ungarisches Lied für Pianoforte

Johannes Brahms, Op. 21, Nr. 2
(Veröffentlicht 1861)

Var. 3

Var. 4

Var. 5 *con espressione*

Var. 6

Var. 7

Poco più lento

p dolce espress.

quasi pizzicato

sostenuto

Ped.

Var. 13

Allegro (il doppio Movimento)

Variationen und Fuge
über ein Thema von Händel für Pianoforte

Johannes Brahms, Op.24
(Veröffentlicht 1862)

Var. 2

Var. 3

Var. 11

Var. 14

Var. 15

Var. 16

Var. 19

leggiero e vivace

Var. 20

Var.24

Var. 25

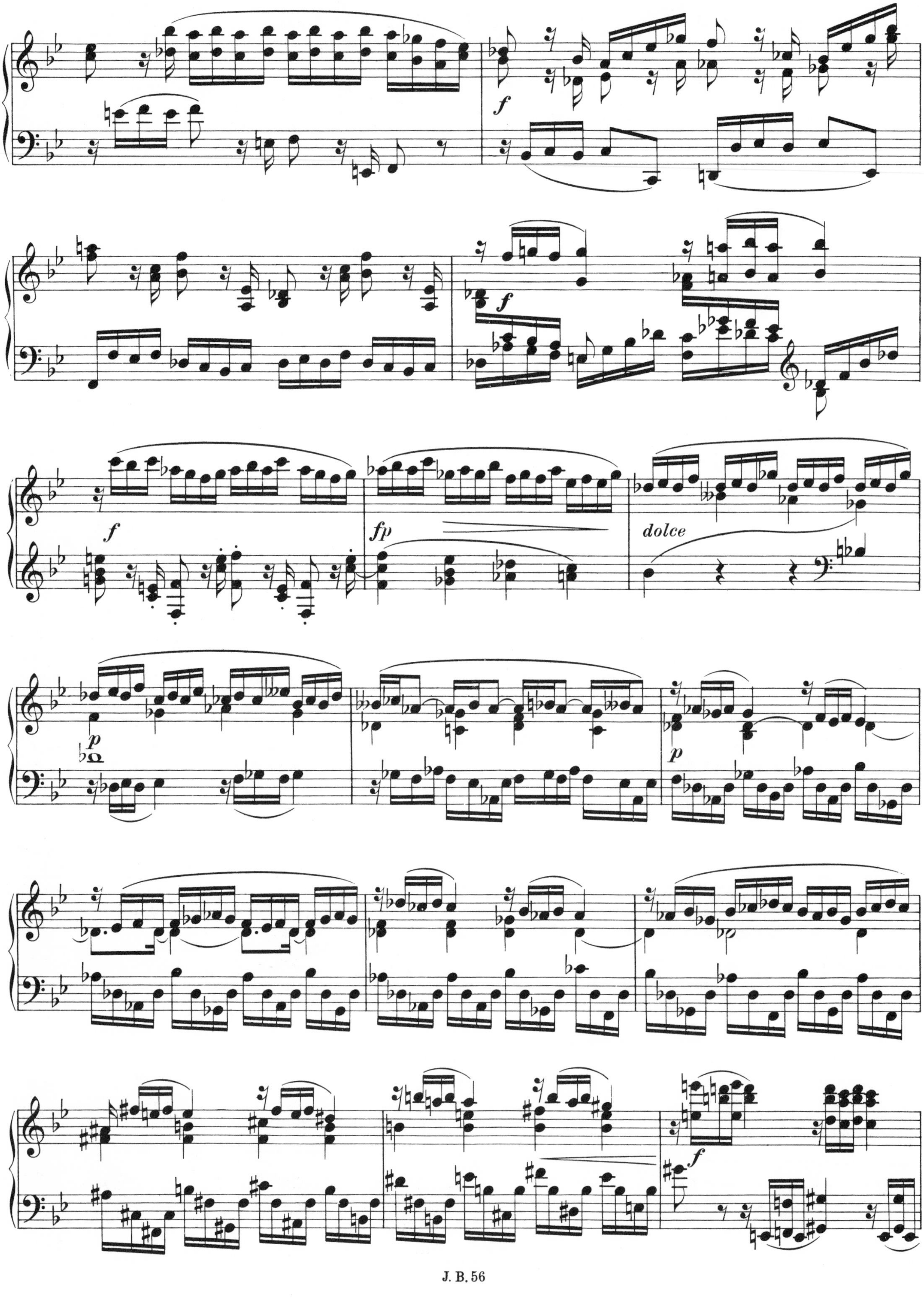
f
f
f
fp
dolce
p
p
f

Studien für Pianoforte
Variationen über ein Thema von Paganini
I.

Thema
Non troppo presto

Johannes Brahms, Op. 35 Heft 1
(Veröffentlicht 1866)

Var. 1

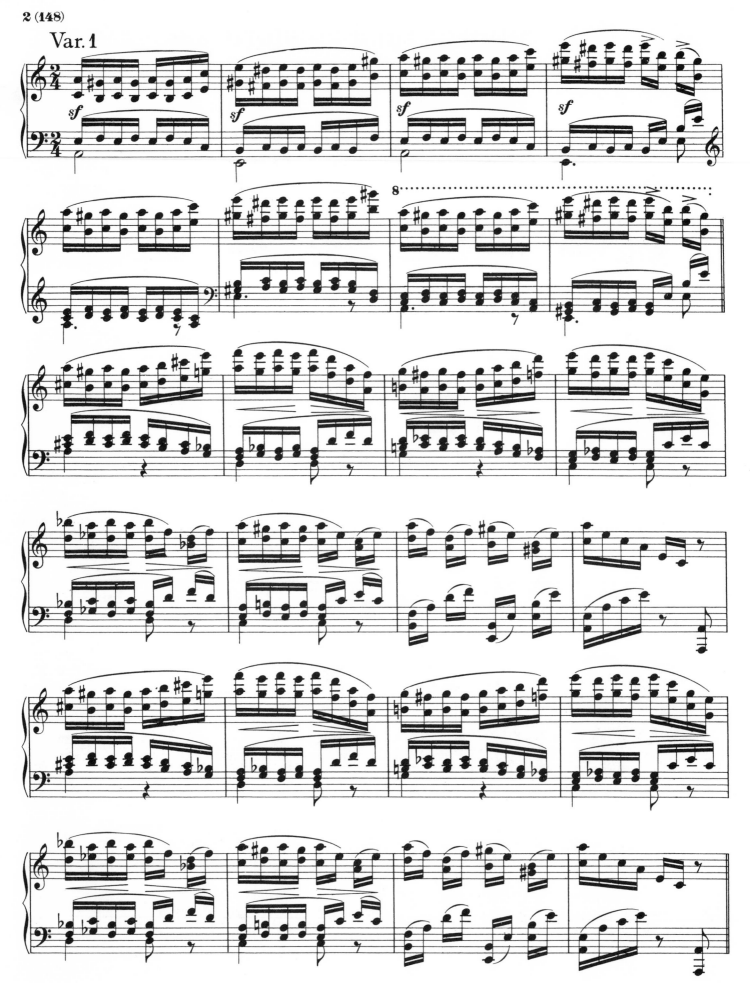

Var. 2

Var. 3

Var. 4

Var. 5

Var. 8

Var. 9

Var. 10

Var. 11

Andante

Var. 12

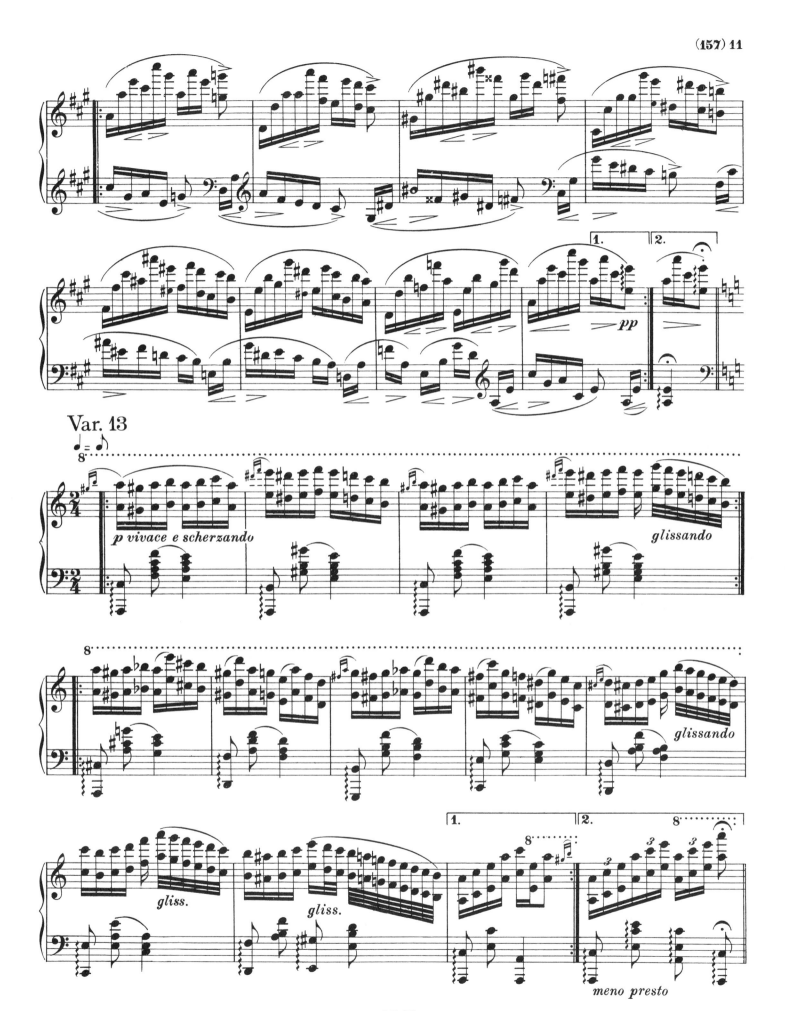

Var. 13

Var. 14
Allegro

Presto, ma non troppo

Studien für Pianoforte
Variationen über ein Thema von Paganini
II.

Johannes Brahms, Op. 35 Heft 2
(Veröffentlicht 1866)

Thema
Non troppo presto

Var.1

Var. 2
Poco animato

Var. 3

Var. 4
Poco Allegretto

Var. 8

Var. 9

J. B. 58

Var. 10
Feroce, energico

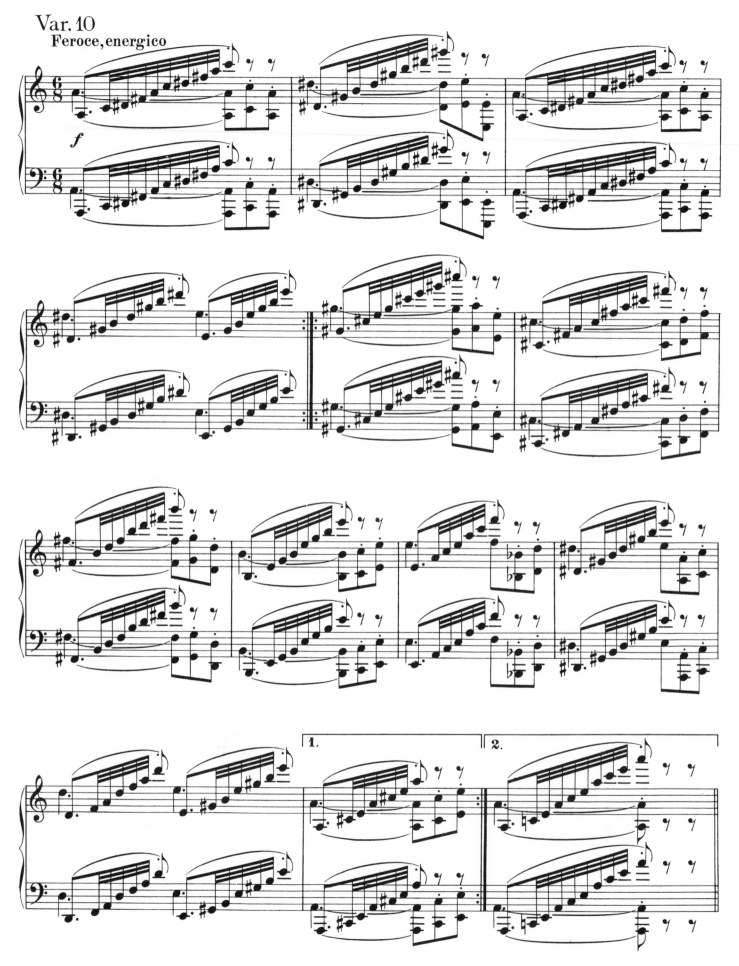

Var. 13

Un poco più Andante

Var. 14

Presto, ma non troppo

p scherzando